SEE THE SIGNS

creating belief, providing hope
affirming connection

KIMBERLY BRAZIER

Copyright © 2023 by Kimberly Brazier
www.KimberlyBrazier.com
www.seethesignsbook.com
All rights reserved.

ISBN: 979-8-218-30123-1

No part of this book may be reproduced, distributed, or transmitted in any form or by any means, including photocopying, recording, or other electronic or mechanical methods, without the prior written permission of the publisher, except in the case of brief quotations embodied in critical articles, reviews, and certain other noncommercial uses permitted by copyright law. This book is not a replacement for therapy or medical advice. If professional assistance is required, the services of a competent professional should be sought. Neither the publisher nor the author shall be liable for the damages that arises here from.

Please note this book may contain accounts that are within the realm of personal belief and interpretation. Ultimately whether one believes in signs is a deeply personal matter influenced by individual beliefs, experiences and cultural perspectives. It is up to the individual to determine the significance and meaning of these experiences in their own lives.

there are signs
appearing in the most unexpected places
creating belief
providing hope
affirming connection
-Kimberly Brazier

For those who are content and those who are curious
For those who believe and those who question
For those who are connected and those who are confused
For those who love deeply and those who are heartbroken
For those who are weary and those who are rested
For those who are calm and those who are anxious
For those who have hope and those who doubt
For those who seek the light and those who are the light

May this book meet you right where you are.
Today.
May it be a reminder as you experience life.
Every day.
May it create belief, provide hope, and affirm connection.
Always.
Much love to you,
Kimberly

With Heartfelt Gratitude

For Sebastian and Briana, my children,
    and my son in law Cameron
For Beckett and Olivia, my grandchildren
For my mom and dad
For my family, including my siblings and their family: Jason, Kristin, Kiley and Jed
For those who opened their hearts to share their stories and photos:
Karyl, Kiley, Kristi, Jackie, Janette, Jed, Jodi, Maureen, Susie
For Jon
For Lisa
For Wendy
For you, the readers, for opening the pages of this book and allowing yourself to See The Signs.

For the unwavering love, encouragement, and belief not only in this book, but in me.
For helping create belief, provide hope and affirm connection.
I am beyond grateful for each and every one of you in my life.
- Kim

CONTENTS

INTRODUCTION	10
ANIMALS	20
COINS	34
DREAMS	38
ELECTRICAL INTERFERENCE	44
FEATHERS	54
MUSIC	64
MOVED OBJECTS	68
NATURE	72
NUMBERS	84
ORBS OF LIGHT	92
PETS AND TODDLERS	100
SIGNS OF PROTECTION	112
WORDS OF AFFIRMATION	118
YOUR PART	124
SIGN STORIES	126
JOURNAL	128

INTRODUCTION

I'd had an early morning, leaving home at 3:30 a.m. in order to arrive at the local airport in time for my 6:05 a.m. flight. The pre-dawn calm made the forty-minute drive feel like an extended moment of solitude, reflection, and gratitude for all that I had.

As my travel day progressed, however, I started to feel uneasy. I couldn't put my finger on why, but I felt like I wanted to be back home. This was unusual for me, as I'd been traveling extensively for work for over six years. I enjoyed my work travel, and while, yes, there were times when I missed home, this was not the same feeling. This time my body was giving me a sign: *go back home*.

Once I arrived at my hotel, though, I couldn't think of any logical reason to disrupt my plans. I was scheduled to meet my customer the following morning and fly out later that day. Certainly, the next twenty-four hours would go quickly, and I would arrive back home before I knew it. A few check-in calls and texts confirmed that my adult children were fine, my parents were fine, my family was fine. So why was I so apprehensive?

Deciding I needed to do something to shake this feeling, I headed over to a Cracker Barrel restaurant close to the hotel. Home-style cooking would surely bring me comfort. As I opened the restaurant's wooden doors and took a step inside, I immediately laughed. To my surprise, the first thing I saw was pink. Pink flamingos. Not just one flamingo but a whole display of them.

In that moment, I knew I was being supported. You see, pink flamingos are my sign from my Grandma J. While holding back the tears, I thought, *Ahhhhh, Grandma J is here. Everything is okay.* She was showing her love and support, watching over me from the other side. My uneasiness was heard, and Grandma J responded. My worries quickly subsided.

Little did I realize that all the signs and messages I was being given during this trip were to prepare me and surround me in love as, less than forty-eight hours later, I experienced one of the most life-changing events I'd ever been through: the unexpected death of my beautiful and loving mother.

God-winks, Synchronicities, and Turning Points

Each of us has turning points in our lives. Out of our life-changing experiences, our times of joy, or our deepest sorrows, we can share our learnings and tools to help support others. Help them in their brightest and darkest hours. Support them in the tiniest and largest decisions. Affirm their belief and give them hope.

Losing my mother was such a turning point for me. This experience brought me tremendous grief, but along with the loving sign I received from Grandma J, it also strengthened my faith and deepened my compassion.

> *I know how weary our souls can feel when we lose someone near and dear to us.*
> *I know how anxious our souls can feel when we're wondering if we're making the right decisions.*
> *I know how tired our souls can feel when we're lost and confused, looking for answers.*

I also know how full of love our souls can feel when we're celebrating gratitude for all the blessings in our life.

And I know how much our souls can ache when we lose that feeling and desperately want it back.

I also know that signs can point the way back to that place of gratitude, joy, and connection.

And I know that, whether we're aware of them, signs are all around us.

The loving sign I received from Grandma J before my mother's passing was just one of a series of messages, God-winks, synchronicities, divine interventions—whatever you may call them—that I've received, documented, and photographed over the past 25 years. As you read this book, you'll experience a small portion of my personal stories and photos of signs that have come along my path when I've asked for guidance, support, comfort, or appeared unexpectedly, yet, at the very right time.

In these pages, you won't find award-winning photography. Instead, you'll find real signs from real life, caught in the moment—photos that were being saved as personal memories. Reminders. Evidence. Photo journals. Although they may not possess the quality of the beautifully curated images we see each day in our social media feeds, even unfiltered, they are still pretty spectacular and sacred to me. I hope you will agree.

In addition to my own collection, I've included some amazing photos and stories from family and friends who've connected to signs in their own lives. After all, I'm certainly not the only person who receives signs. I genuinely believe that you've been receiving them as well. Perhaps you've already noticed them. But if not, be prepared. Your life is about to change for the better!

An Invitation

As you turn the pages of this book, I invite you to remember that you are not forgotten and you are not alone. I invite you to dwell on the possibility of experiencing these magical connections for yourself. And I invite you to remember that you are indeed connected to someone and something miraculous—something unseen that can be affirmed by signs.

>So, are you ready?
>Ready to open your mind to creating belief?
>Ready to open your soul to providing hope?
>Ready to open your heart to affirming connection?
>Let's go, loves. Let's go! Let's experience it together.
>Let me guide you to ***see the signs***.

What Is a Sign?

According to Google, a sign is "an object, quality, or event whose presence or occurrence indicates the probable presence or occurrence of something else." That seems like a good definition for us to begin with. But what do these presences or occurrences mean?

Signs can be interpreted in many ways. Some people, including myself, think that signs are messages from a higher power, such as God, angels, or a loved one who's passed away. They can alert us to someone or something significant, such as an upcoming experience or a special person in our lives.

Signs can come in many forms, such as a sudden feeling of warmth, a song on the radio, a vivid dream, or even a physical object that appears unexpectedly. What may be a sign to one person may not be a sign to another, and each person may interpret signs in their own way. A sign could be seen as a message of guidance, comfort, or love. Or it could mean that someone is wanting you to know you were important in their life and that they desire to connect with you. Just as you may feel the need to connect with them, they may also long to connect with you.

Don't get caught up in the perception that signs only come in a certain form. Some may think signs are big, bold, and grand. So audacious you couldn't miss it. Which, may be true at times. However, I find there is often a simplicity to a sign. Generally, right there, all by itself. Standing alone for your attention. So simple you may pass it by not thinking much about it. As you'll see from the numerous examples in this book, the ways in which they may appear is endless. Seeing a sign doesn't require any one particular item or experience; however, it does require belief and an open mind.

Asking for a Sign

Asking for a sign is a very simple process. You don't have to do anything overly complicated. Try using a method that you may already have established in your daily life.

- You can pray.
- You can meditate.
- You can light a candle.
- You can write a letter.
- You can talk to a departed loved one, either out loud or silently in your mind.
- You can ask to receive a sign through a dream.
- Or you can simply trust that one will appear.

Everything is a vibration, a frequency. So however, you choose to ask for signs, your words and thoughts express a frequency that can be heard and understood by the unseen.

Here are some examples of words and phrases you can use to ask for a sign:

- Dear (loved one's name), I miss you so much. If you're here with me, please give me a sign.
- Dear (loved one's name), please let me know that you're okay. Please give me a sign that you're at peace.
- I'm feeling so happy and excited for what just happened in my life. (Insert name of higher power, loved one, or angel), did you see what just happened? If so, please send me a sign.
- I need some reassurance that I can make it through what I'm encountering now. Can you please send me a sign to let

me know that you're still with me, supporting me through this?
- Please show me a (insert the sign you want to see). This sign means so much to me.

These are just examples, and you should feel free to use your own words and express yourself in a way that feels like you—the authentic, wonderful, beautiful soul you are. Express your request in a way that your higher power or loved one would connect with, just as if they were on the phone with you or sitting right beside you.

Do You Know What Signs to Look For?

In this book, I can't highlight every sign that anyone has seen or connected to; however, I will focus on the most common types of signs that I've seen, heard about, or researched.

Each sign may have a different specific meaning to everyone, including yourself. After all, your connection to your loved ones, a higher power, or the angelic realm is individualized. It's a connection that no one else holds or understands as uniquely and powerfully as you do.

ANIMALS

All things bright and beautiful,
All creatures great and small,
All things wise and wonderful,
The Lord God made them all.

– Cecil Frances Alexander

Cardinals and butterflies and deer oh my!

The animal kingdom is estimated to encompass 3–30 million species as of 2022. Can you imagine that? In addition to enriching our planet and preserving the balance of life, these animals can also send us messages.

When you see a specific animal repeatedly, unexpectedly, or synchronously, this may be a sign for you. You may notice the animal right next to your window for long periods of time, flying around you, or landing on you. It may appear out of nowhere or in unusual spots. Or you may see an animal that a loved one who has passed had a special connection with.

Oftentimes, loved ones will share what animal they want to appear as and communicate with us from the other side. When you see that special animal, I encourage to you pause and connect. Acknowledge their presence. Say hello. Talk to them. Thank them for coming. Ask them for any messages they have for you. And invite them to come back and visit again.

Although signs may appear through actual animals, you may also spot them in other forms. Just as I saw a shelf full of pink flamingos, you may find your animal sign on an inanimate object, such as an advertisement, a mug, a T-shirt, or a literal sign displaying your animal. The options are endless! Keep your eyes open.

Hummingbirds, butterflies, cardinals, deer, rabbits, squirrels blue jays, owls, hawks, dragonflies, ladybugs, cats, and dogs are some of the top reported animal signs.

What animals have you noticed showing up around you?

Are there certain animals that you feel connected to?

How do you feel when you experience an animal sign?

Mikey and the Cat

My daughter Bree shared her birthday with her friend Mikey. They were in some of the same high school classes, walked their dogs together, did teenage things together. Over time, they developed a strong bond. They were so connected that one night while they were out for dinner, they decided to draw a picture for each other—and drew practically the same scene! But their connection went well beyond such external coincidences. They shared a passion for life, a kindness to others, and a love that they radiated in their own unique ways. I credit it to them both being born on the day of love: Valentine's Day.

The day before we left for my daughter's college orientation in June 2013, we found out that Mikey had crossed to the other side.

That fall Bree attended a college out of state, approximately three hours away. On Friday evenings she would occasionally carpool home with other college kids from our local area. As I was anticipating her first arrival back home since being away at college, I noticed a tabby cat sitting on our doorstep. We didn't have a cat, and neither did any of our neighbors. I'd never seen that cat before. Strange, I thought.

When Bree arrived back home, the cat was still there on the doorstep to greet her. Bree immediately said, "Mom, it's Mikey!" Mikey loved tabby cats. In fact, Bree had gotten a cat tattoo on her foot to memorialize Mikey.

After her visit, when Bree returned to college, the cat seemed to disappear. It wasn't around for a few weeks until, you guessed it, Bree was about to arrive back home again. This time, after waiting at the doorstep for a while, the cat moved to my deck, where it meowed at the sliding glass door to get my attention. My daughter's ride home was running late and thus her arrival was late. For hours, the cat sat on the deck, meowing on and off, pawing anxiously at the sliding glass door, and looking at me as if he was worried about her, asking where she was. The cat was actually making me worried about Bree's delayed arrival. I talked to the cat and said, "Bree is still coming, just later than anticipated." He remained on a steadfast watch until Bree arrived, when he immediately ran down the deck steps and right up to her.

Bree has had many "Mikey cat" sightings through the years as her sign from him. Each time very meaningful. Mikey was a blessing in her life and continues to be a protector and connector from the other side. Mostly recently, while reading this section of the book to Bree while working on edits, a tabby cat appeared on the steps outside my front door. My neighbor asked me later that day if I had gotten a cat. I smiled and said no.

The cardinal is looking toward my sister, Kiley, who often sees cardinals as a sign.

Cardinals

You may be familiar with the saying, when cardinals appear angels are near. Cardinals are often associated with loved ones who have passed away, watching over you and returning for a visit. Often seen as a symbol of renewal and transformation, they are believed to represent the cycle of life, death, and rebirth. Overall, cardinals are seen as a positive and uplifting symbol, representing hope, love, and spirituality. They serve as a reminder that loved ones can never truly be forgotten.

I'd love to share some amazing stories about cardinals with you, however my experiences and others are that cardinals appear. Simply and quietly appear. Often you are gazing outside or looking up and there is a bright red coat of hope staring back at you. It is as if they swoop in at the most divine time. They linger and allow time for you to notice them, connect with them and communicate with them. This may ring true for other birds as well such as blue jays, robins, mourning doves, owls, hummingbirds, and hawks.

Deer

While on my way back from running errands one fall day in 2015, I was thinking how nice it would be to have coffee, cookies, and homemade buns and cheese sandwiches with Grandpa J, Grandma J, and Grandma B one more time. Suddenly I had an urge to drive through our old neighborhood. Imagine my surprise when I saw these three as I rounded the corner into the residential neighborhood. Seeing these deer made me feel closer to my grandparents, I felt as if their spirit was there with me. Although our loved ones may have been gone for years, there is no expiration date on connections with them.

While this is not the only time I have seen the three of them together through the years, it was a great reminder for me to set my intention and listen to my intuition. Deciding to drive through our old neighborhood made no sense at the time, but it made all the sense in the world once I saw the three of them.

In April 2023, shortly after I moved, my deer gang appeared back in action. Early one morning I was making the forty-minute drive back to my previous home to finish the moving process. I had many boxes to move, some cupboards yet to pack up, curtain rods to take down, an entire house to clean from top to bottom to name just a few of my remaining tasks before the movers arrived the following day. In the moment, it seemed insurmountable.

My mind was running frantically with all kinds of thoughts. Could I accomplish all I needed to? Would I have enough time? Could I do it all alone? Had I truly made the right decision? If this chapter of my life was closing, what amazing things would be unfolding for me next?

My mind rambled on as quickly as my driving. Then I paused for a moment and thought, *Stop worrying! Ask for a sign.* So, I did. I asked for a sign to confirm I could handle everything I needed to do alone and that, yes indeed, I had made the right decision.

I entered the house and got to work taping up boxes to fill with my belongings. No longer than an hour had passed when, as I was moving boxes from the house to the garage, something outside the large picture window caught my eye—something running on the frozen-over lake outside the house. Wait, what was that? I looked again and saw three deer running toward my house. I screamed with excitement, "Oh my gosh! There they are!"

I frantically tried to find my phone. Luckily, I was able to grab it, take a few photos, and record a video. During my photo shoot, the deer graciously stopped running and looked right at me, posing motionlessly as I peered at them through my window.

Then, after a few minutes, they playfully began to run around one another. Eventually, they turned around and ran away in the direction they came from.

It brought tears to my eyes to know that my request was heard. Not once in the three and a half years that I had lived on the lake had I seen any wild animal run freely on the ice. What were they even doing on the ice when it was melting season? While it seemed to make no sense, again, I just knew they were my sign that, yes, I could handle this move and I had made the right decision. My anxious mind had its answers.

Deer are known for their grace and gentleness. Seeing one can be a reminder of your loved one's gentle nature. Deer are seen as protectors. Seeing a deer can be a sign that your loved one is looking out and offering you protection and comfort. As deer shed and regrow their antlers each year, seeing a deer may indicate that you are experiencing a new beginning or entering a new phase of your life. Their presence is a way of offering guidance and support as you navigate your life.

Photo credit Jon Flatland

Butterflies

My dear friend Jackie shared with me this beautiful glimpse of a butterfly sign her children and family members experienced.

In the summer of 2008, siblings Greta and Jeremy Nelson had a surprising and magical encounter with a butterfly. Their nineteen-year-old cousin Brady had passed away unexpectedly in the summer two years earlier, and he was making his presence known and saying hello during his family's annual weekend at the lake. When the butterfly landed first on Brady's dad, Brady's stepmom said right away "It's Brady!" The butterfly then landed and lingered on seven more relatives, which brought pure joy and connection to the family that day.

Butterflies are known for their transformative journey from a caterpillar to a beautiful butterfly. Seeing a butterfly can represent a message of transformation and rebirth, reminding you that your loved one is now in a new form and at peace. Butterflies can represent the love you shared with your loved one and the connection you still have them even though they're no longer physically present. Seeing a butterfly, a butterfly can be a sign that your loved one's spirit is nearby, watching over you, offering guidance and support as you navigate through life without them.

COINS

*So don't pass by that penny when you're feeling blue.
It may be a penny from heaven that an angel's passed to you.*

– Charles Marshburn

Discovering coins could be your sign. Sometimes believed to be pennies (or nickels, dimes, or quarters) sent from the heavens, coins may appear for you as a gesture from a guardian angel or cherished loved one or to signify good luck. I feel that discovering a coin is confirmation that a loved one wants to share how much they love and value you.

Coins can appear in your path, on your counters or floors. When you come across a coin, don't simply pick it up and put it into your change container or pocket. Hold onto it for a moment. Look at the year on the coin. This year may represent a sentimental date. It could be the year of a birth, death, or some other memorable event.

Coins are commonly known as currency and also can be referred to as change. If you have been desiring reassurance that change is needed in your life or that you are headed in the right direction with the changes you've made, remain observant for coins that you find their way to you.

A penny for your thoughts…could coins be a sign you haven't recognized yet?

Pay attention to how often you're finding and picking up coins.

Just as coins have value, so do you. If you didn't already know, you are priceless!

Your memories of your loved ones are priceless too.

Pennies found on counter tops and floors appear, even after I have cleaned my house and those surfaces. Do you find coins in strange places or space they weren't before?

Surprise finds: two dimes in the middle of the hotel room floor that hadn't been there before. I discovered these while on a work trip, confirming that my work was of value that day.

DREAMS

> *I close my eyes, then I drift away*
> *into the magic night I softly say*
> *a silent prayer, like dreamers do,*
> *then I fall asleep to dream my dreams of you.*
>
> — Roy Orbison

It was so real! That's what you might feel as you awake from a vivid dream of a passed loved one.

Our loved ones may appear in dreams to share a message or to offer comfort. They may reassure you that they're okay and are still with you in spirit. Sometimes they appear in symbolic form, such as one of the signs being shared in this book, or as an image that represents them or their message. Other times they may appear through a dream about an experience you shared, such as a favorite activity or a place that you both enjoyed. Most often they appear as themselves as they looked when they were alive and healthy.

My son recently called me and shared that he'd had a dream where my mom (his grandma) and he had sat down and had a cup of tea. She wanted to know what was going on in his life and how he was doing. This dream felt like real life to him. In actuality, this is exactly what she did when she was here on earth and, most likely, would have done with him again.

Sometimes our dreams are simply a reflection of our own thoughts and feelings. But if you have a dream that *feels real*, that *feels significant*, trust your intuition that your loved one did indeed visit you. Pause and reflect on the dream's meaning or what your loved one may be trying to communicate to you. Don't forget to check your clock! Take note of the time you awoke from your dream end. Did it conclude at a magical number sequence such as 4:44? Do you experience the dreams at the same time each time they occur?

Don't put this book down yet, in the upcoming chapter on orbs of light, I share a repetitive dream I had and how it was a sign for someone else.

If you wake up after an impactful dream, why not record your experience?

Keep a journal and pen next to your bed to capture details and feelings from your dream.

Use your phone to create a voice recording detailing the dream.

By documenting these amazing occurrences right after they happen, you are creating a memory to honor and reflect on.

ELECTRICAL INTERFERENCE

Don't you know yet?
It's your light that lights the world.

– Rumi

Have you ever noticed garage doors opening unexpectedly or door bells ringing with no one there? Maybe you have light bulbs flickering, turning on and off, or perhaps they brighten and dim or burn out frequently? Have you heard static interference when listening to a radio or noticed your cell phone going wonky? Computers freezing up on you? These may be a few ways spirits can manipulate or tap into electrical energy and make their presence known.

There is a belief that the spirit of loved ones can manifest their presence through electrical interference in our lives. These unexplained electrical phenomena are perceived as a way for loved ones to establish a connection with the physical world and communicate their presence or provide comfort and guidance.

If this surprises you, consider that everything is energy. You are energy, electricity is energy, and spirits are energy.

It's important to know that these experiences are highly personal. While some people find solace in interpreting these electrical interferences as signs, others may attribute them to coincidences or natural explanations. As you continue to immerse yourself in this book, I will let you determine how you feel about current chaos.

Are you plugged in to spotting electrical signs?

In July 2016, I had a workday that was challenging, to put it mildly. You know the days when everything seems to be falling apart—or burning down—and you wonder how much more can you take? It had been one of those days. Somehow, though, I made it five o'clock.

As I was waiting for the elevator to leave for the day, I paused and asked God to show me the light so I could get through another day tomorrow. Suddenly, before the elevator doors could even open, bright lights began flashing in unison with a blaring noise—a fire alarm! It was as if I was being shown that even amid what I was feeling on that fiery day, the light is always there to guide me.

SEE THE SIGNS

Be open to seeing the light during challenging days.

Can you be the light for others when they need a sign?

Heaven Is for Real

Unexpected loss can be devastating, but it can also create a deeper connection to family and friends. My aunt Karyl and I had numerous conversations in the midst of grief, recalling joyful memories and sharing signs that each of us had received. Karyl shared the following story about her sister (my mother):

My sister Barb passed away unexpectedly. I was inconsolable; I couldn't imagine losing my only sister. A few days after she died, I asked her to send me a sign. It could be anything. I just needed her to let me know she was okay. Of course, I wanted an immediate result and was disappointed when it didn't come. Two days later, I turned on the television and a banner came across the screen with the name of the movie that was playing: *Heaven Is for Real*. I couldn't believe it There it was; Barb had given me my sign.

Mom's calling

(Shared by my brother Jed)

I lost my mom about ten months ago, as of this writing. I miss her often and dearly.

For background's sake, I don't personally subscribe to any organized religion, nor do I find one any more particularly credible than the next one, and I don't believe in heaven. That said, I do think there is more to the universe that we don't understand than that we do, and I like to think that when we die, whatever it is that makes us "us"—call it our soul, spirit, consciousness, energy, whatever—does move on. Maybe we end up on the other side of the dimensional veil in a whole new place we can't begin to comprehend, or maybe we all end up returning to a collective source where it all first sprang from in the first place.

Now, sure, maybe there is "nothing" when we die, just life's off-switch being flipped, and maybe the above is just a nice idea for someone who misses a loved one, hasn't fully processed their grief, and is still in mourning—a brain short-circuiting its logic board to try to soothe a hurting heart—but I don't think so. I think there is more. And if we keep our hearts, minds, and eyes open, there are signs…some perhaps less subtle than others.

Not that long ago, the first morning in a long while that I hadn't found myself actively missing mom during my first hour of being awake, I left for work the same as I always do: laptop bag over my shoulder, keys in my hand, slipping my phone into the chest pocket of my shirt as I headed out the back door. I walked to the garage, climbed into my SUV, and drove to work per usual. It was textbook "ordinary."

Once I got to the office, I pulled out my iPhone to turn on a podcast, and instead of the usual home screen, it showed the search bar, and in the search field, it displayed three letters: "Mom" at 8:23 am.

I don't use Siri—I've never even set that feature up on my phone—or any voice-to-text functions. I hadn't spoken to anyone that morning in person, and I didn't call anyone on the drive to work. I didn't use my phone at all that morning other than to glance at it to see what time it was when I first woke up. I hadn't actually touched the screen at all that morning, but there it was: "Mom."

And what's more, it wouldn't go away. I couldn't X out of the search function; I couldn't swipe it away. It wouldn't do anything other than show "Mom." Odd as it was, I showed it to my coworker and asked if she could close out of it. She couldn't and said "spooky," which was less amusing in the moment than I think it is now, though looking back, I am fortunate to at least have had a witness.

After verifying that she too saw "Mom" and was also unable get my phone to respond, I went back to my office, sat at my desk, and took a screenshot. I'm not sure why, honestly. While it has come to mean a lot more, at the time it was more of a "Well, this is weird and someone else should see this" than an "Okay, I see you."

I took an intentional breath, pictured my smiling mother, and made a conscious effort to send her a message: "Good morning, Mom. I miss you too."

Aside from momentarily leaky eyes and a brief lump in my throat, that was it. I restarted my phone and was left with nothing but a screenshot and an unusual story. The rest of the day was just as textbook "ordinary" as the morning had started out. I wish I could tell you there were seven other signs from Mom that day to really make it a truly miraculous "from beyond the grave "story, but there weren't.

I have since thought a lot about that morning, about what that could mean. I may never know if it was more than a random phone glitch or a one-in-twenty-six-to-the-third-power chance that somehow, some way my phone typed "Mom" without me noticing I brushed up against my shirt pocket even though it was facing away from me and behind two layers of fabric.

Maybe it's all just cosmic dominoes falling where they may, coincidences simply playing tricks with our powerful feelings, messing with our brains because humans are emotional creatures who excel at storytelling and all too often being overly self-focused. But in this case, I do think it was a sign.

Just not the one I thought initially.

I think at least sometimes that when we see a sign, it isn't appearing just because of a phantom memory of someone we care about randomly bubbling up from our subconscious or us reminiscing about a loved one who is no longer in our lives and we're "just" missing them. Maybe—just maybe—we see the sign because sometimes *they* miss *us*.

FEATHERS

Feathers appear when angels are near.
(unknown source)

I am a self-proclaimed feather finder. Feathers tend to be one of my signs I find very frequently—so frequently I could add it to my resume under skills. I likely could have dedicated this whole book to photos of the various feathers and their stories. However, don't think that I'm claiming to see feathers just to say that I've received another sign. They truly do flock to me, showing up in the most amazing and fun places, under many different circumstances, and in a wide variety of sizes, textures, and colors.

In many cultures throughout history, feathers have been considered a symbol of spirituality and communication with the divine. Many people believe that feathers are a sign that our loved ones are still with us, watching us from the spiritual realm. Feathers remind me of the wings that some angels are thought to have. They are God's messengers and serve as protection, guidance, and human assistance. Whether you find a feather on your usual path or in an unexpected place, you indeed might be a member of the feather-finder club too!

What size and color feathers do you find?

Who in your family flock could be sharing feathers with you as a sign?

SEE THE SIGNS 57

In the fall of 2019 I called my sister about some strange things happening such as dishes falling out of my cupboard, and a lost debit card even though I hadn't left the car with it. I laughed and said "whatever happened to me finding feathers? I just need a sign! "And the minute I stepped out of my car there was this feather. Even though I can't explain how this magic works, I truly love signs like this.

When you pull out your tea tree oil and you find a sign,
A much-needed sign,
At a time when it takes every ounce to get through the day,
Every single ounce of hope and a moment or two to pray,
You know, the kind of day that is filled with tears running down your face
And you are trying to find something to embrace,
Releasing the expectations you once had
While wondering when you will not feel so bad,
When no one seems to notice how you feel,
Making it seem like this life cannot be real,
And then you glance down again and see
The sign that gives you the support that is meant to be.

SEE THE SIGNS

I previously shared this story fall of 2017 in the bestselling book "Goodness Abounds -365 True Stories of Loving Kindness."

The August heat and humidity weighed heavily on my body, but the words spoken by my brother sent a chill down my spine. "Dad had a heart attack." My father had already gone through one life or death heart attack situation 20 years earlier, so I knew this one would be a challenge as well. Sometimes being in the healthcare field is helpful and other times your knowledge can be dangerously real when it comes to situations like this.

After sharing what was unfolding on social media, a community of hundreds gathered in virtual prayer. Isn't it amazing that with one tap of a computer button, we can click on the power of prayer?

Spending time at the bedside of my father in the ICU those first few days led to worry and concern. When I stepped out for a quick bite to eat, I asked for a sign that all would be well.

At a gas station near the hospital, the aroma of fresh baked bread filled the air. My father's mother was known for her homemade bread and buns. I commented on the delicious smell and even though it was not yet packaged for sale, the clerk kindly offered some to me. It felt as if my grandmother was telling us she was there alongside us.

Our hopes were deflated by a surgeon who felt my father's condition made it too risky to perform the surgery. It occurred to me that maybe the situation required a fresh set up eyes- those of a surgeon who held a strong belief in his ability to return a damaged heart to optimal function. Sure enough, our request for another doctor's opinion led us to that surgeon.

Later that day, I noticed a feather on the floor in the family lounge. A sign from the Divine, leaving me with a feeling that my dad was in good hands.

This is the feather found August 24, 2016 (thank you Angels) on the second floor of a hospital, Yep that's crazy right? It was located outside the ICU where my dad had been for 12 days and recovering from high-risk bypass surgery. It was a journey of trusting and asking for support. All turned out amazing well.

MUSIC

Music gives a soul to the universe, wings to the mind, flight to the imagination, and life to everything.

– Plato

Turn up the radio! Music has the power to evoke strong emotions and memories. We can receive messages of guidance from song lyrics, or loved ones can let us know they are still with us by playing a song. You may hear a particular song that you relate to a loved one, often at significant moments or at times when you're thinking of them.

Father-daughter dance music, a prom-night theme song, or a song you always sang together may come on the radio as you enter your car. A song with lyrics that include your loved one's name may catch your ear. You may be walking through a store and hear a melody that's so catchy that you and a loved one once rolled down the windows and sang it at the top of your lungs, smiling and giggling all the while. Songs you danced to all night or the ones that you just *felt* the words emotionally may start playing out of nowhere. Perhaps it was an opera, Broadway musical, country or rock music concert or festival you attended together, and the memory of time spent together is provoked again by the music. Perhaps every station you tune into is playing a song you once sang while sitting around a campfire with loved ones. Did you two claim a song as *your* song? Maybe that's the song you hear repeatedly.

When I am chatting with my girlfriend, we often get deep into life conversations about what is or is not happening in our lives. I am always surprised at the songs she sends me to listen to and how the lyrics are exactly what I need to hear. It's like the artist had just produced their music for me and a sign is being sent to me through her. If you are hearing a song over and over, especially if it is not a top hit on the radio, pay attention to the lyrics. What do they mean or represent to you at this time in your life?

Take time to listen. Listen with an open mind and open ears.

What lyrics are guiding you when you're searching for answers?

I encourage you to go play a favorite song that reminds you of your loved one.

MOVED OBJECTS

The objects that we find are vessels of memories and remnants of their presence that keep their spirit alive with us. In our hands and in our hearts forever.

-Kimberly Brazier

Objects have a strange way of manifesting in the most unexpected locations. You may find items moved from its original location and you begin to wonder how it got there. It is believed that these subtle actions serve as a sign or a means of communication from a deceased loved one. A moved object can seem a bit disruptive and yet it catches your attention that someone may be trying to connect with you.

Objects we find from our deceased loved ones often hold deep emotional significance. They serve as tangible reminders of the person. They hold a unique power to evoke memories, and a sense of connection to our loved ones.

These objects can vary greatly in nature, from personal belongings such as clothing, jewelry or accessories to cherished heirlooms, photographs, handwritten letters or cards or even everyday items. Each object carries a story, a piece of history, a fragment of their life. These objects can also become cherished keepsakes, treasured mementoes that we hold near and dear to our heart. They often get passed down through generations. These objects can offer a sense of comfort and keep their spirit alive within us.

Have you ever found an object out of place and wondered why? Or how?

Are there special items you found that belonged to a loved one?

How did you feel when you connected with that item?

SEE THE SIGNS

Shared by my friend Susie Boushee

I would like to share with you my story about my friend Derek. He was a friend whom I met in Duluth Minnesota in 1991. He was humorous, giving and most of all the most caring person I know. Derek had moved from Minnesota to North Carolina, and we stayed in touch. He would often visit in the warm summer months. Derek had a zest for life, never missed a card for my birthday or a gift for the holidays. About four years ago he informed me he had melanoma. My immediate response as a nurse was how can I fix it? Knowing that was not possible, I did what a friend does, I supported, listened and laughed with my friend throughout his journey. Then I received a call that Derek had passed away. I remember it clearly. I was visiting my friend at one of the most peaceful places for me, the North Shore of Minnesota.

After I gathered myself from the news, I went for a walk to talk to Derek and seek solace in knowing that he was no longer suffering. Looking down on the dirt path, what do I see? A $100 bill. I was with a friend and asked her " do you see this? Is this real?" And it was. All I could think of was Derek somehow did that. He was a jokester and this was his way of easing my sadness and providing me a laugh. I have kept that hundred dollar bill as a sign that Derek is with me.

I do believe in signs are all around us, I see cardinals on my morning walks and find dimes in the oddest of places. To me these are signs or "gifts" from Derek assuring me he is with me on my walk here on earth My wish for you is to see the signs of loved ones who have passed and feel the warmth and love from beyond.

NATURE

If you truly love nature, you will find beauty everywhere.

Vincent Van Gogh

Nature is often used as a connection from a divine power or loved ones because it is seen as a universal language that transcends cultural and religious boundaries. Nature is a powerful force that can inspire feelings of awe, wonder, and joy and can remind us of the beauty and mystery of life. It can help us tap deeper into finding meaning and purpose during uncertainty or grief. The healing power of nature lightens depression, allows us to clear our mind, restores happiness, and enhances our connection to something larger.

    Our days are busy coming and going. Are you being present with your surroundings as you walk to your car, into work or attending kids activities? Slowing down your pace and glancing in all directions including down, widens your view of your surroundings. No matter what the season- winter, spring, summer of fall- you can almost always find beauty, peacefulness and inspiration in nature. And maybe, just maybe, a sign or two.

Step outside, bask in all the elements of nature and discover the beauty of signs.

Go on now, what are you waiting for?

My friend Kristi Bergstrom shared one of her amazing sign stories with me.

Kristi lost her son Pierce in a tragic accident months before he was to graduate college. They both were avid runners, even competing in marathons together. Kristi's son was killed on August 15; however, the family wasn't notified of the tragedy until the next day.

The following day, while out for a run processing her grief, Kristi found this single rose on the running path. The landscape where she was running does not have any type of flowers, certainly not roses. But what could be a more heartfelt connection than a son sending his mom a sign in the form of a rose, a spiritual symbol of enduring love.

Kristi found this rose on August 17, which is also her youngest son's birthday and only twenty-four hours after she'd received the horrific news—reinforcement that there is no waiting period for signs to appear. Time does not exist in the afterlife; it is a human concept.

Rainbows

I photographed this rainbow captured outside my home during a conversation with my daughter. In the midst of discussing life's hardships and joys, I was giving her motherly advice and support, reassuring her that all would be fine. I saw this rainbow as confirmation, a sign of hope.

Bloom Where You are Planted

My aunt Karyl L. shared this story with me.

My mother, Mavis, was an avid gardener. Most days found her outside working in her flower beds. All of Mom's flowers grew and bloomed beautifully except for one. It came up every year, grew tall and broad, and had beautiful foliage, but it never bloomed, no matter what she did.

When Mom passed away, I took some of her flowers to transplant at my own home. I wanted to carry on her legacy. Included among the perennials I took was the elusive one that refused to bloom. Unfortunately, it seemed to be growing the same way for me as it had for her.

During one particularly difficult day when I was really missing my mom, I asked God for a sign that she was okay and was near me. A few days later, I went to my flowerbed, and I couldn't believe it—the plant that had never bloomed before had a beautiful pink flower. I had received my sign; God had heard my plea. I knew then that mom was fine and near me. That plant has bloomed every year since.

Angel in the Fountain

Janette Stuart and her family were on a trip to celebrate her aunt and uncle's fiftieth wedding anniversary at the Butchart Gardens. When she saw the fountain and the gorgeous spring flowers, she wanted to take a photo. When she took the photo, the fountain sprayed up, and her aunt exclaimed, "It looks like an angel!" This was perfect for their magical day together celebrating love.

I continue to be in awe every time I look at this photo. Did you spot the angel and include its wings in the photo? The amazingness of this photo creates a renewed belief.

Heart Shapes in Nature

Hearts found in nature could signify someone is thinking of you. A sign of love, joy, and compassion, it reminds us that we are all connected—here on earth and beyond. Love has no boundaries. Discovering heart-shaped objects may bring you a sense of peace and a feeling of being loved. May you realize that each step you take, you are supported by love. And I guarantee that, if nothing else, spotting hearts will at least make you smile.

Our days are busy coming and going. Are you being present with your surroundings as you walk to your car, into to work or the grocery store or to attend kids activities? Slowing down your pace and glancing in all directions including down, widens the view of your surroundings. No matter what the season- winter, spring, summer or fall- you can almost always find beauty, peacefulness or inspiration in nature.

While out walking, I've stumbled across the heart shapes on the next pages: a yellow heart leaf, the fallen heart nut from a tree, hearts on a sidewalk, and a small metal heart. These are just a few examples of heart-shaped varieties I've encountered along my path. I was definitely feeling the love on those days.

Time to play hide and seek.

Seek to find three signs in nature.

Now that you're aware of the possibility of signs,

you may notice that they weren't hiding from you after all.

Arrows Point the Way

Ever been looking for confirmation that you're headed in the right direction? Me too. Arrows shown in these photos may be interpreted as that I was going in the right direction. Notice how they're both facing forward, as if to tell me to keep going on my current path. I did, and well, here I am today sharing these signs with you. Are you starting to see how abundant signs are?

NUMBERS

Everything is magical when you see it with your heart.

-Mooji

Have you ever looked at your phone or a clock and seen the numbers 11:11? Shh…I won't tell anyone, but how many of you make a wish when you see those numbers?

Numbers repeating are those that have the same digits, one following after the other in succession, such as 111, 222, 333, or 444 and so on. Some call these angel numbers. Some people believe that these numbers are signs that angels or spirit guides are trying to get your attention or communicate with you. Perhaps they are trying to send a message, such as that you are right where you are supposed to be at that time and that you are in alignment with your life.

I take notice when I see repeating numbers or number sequences. It is exciting and mysterious when they appear on phones, odometers, license plates, store receipts. You may see them in addresses, phone numbers and on the likes received on social media posts, endless places they can appear. For years I have looked up repeating numbers and number sequences online to see what their potential meanings are. There are numerous websites that focus solely on this topic, breaking down combination after combination of numbers. Feel free to check them out and see how to correspond to what you feel they mean for you.

As I mentioned earlier, each sign can be a unique message to the individual, don't forget so can these numbers. When you see these numbers repeatedly, pause and reflect on how you feel. Do the numbers have specific reference or importance in your life? Are they indicative of a birth date, a death, a house number, a lucky number? Maybe it's a jersey number a loved one wore playing sports, the options are endless. It's meaning is for you to uncover and you alone.

Is there a number pattern you see regularly?

Have you determined what it means to you?

What unique number sequences do you experience?

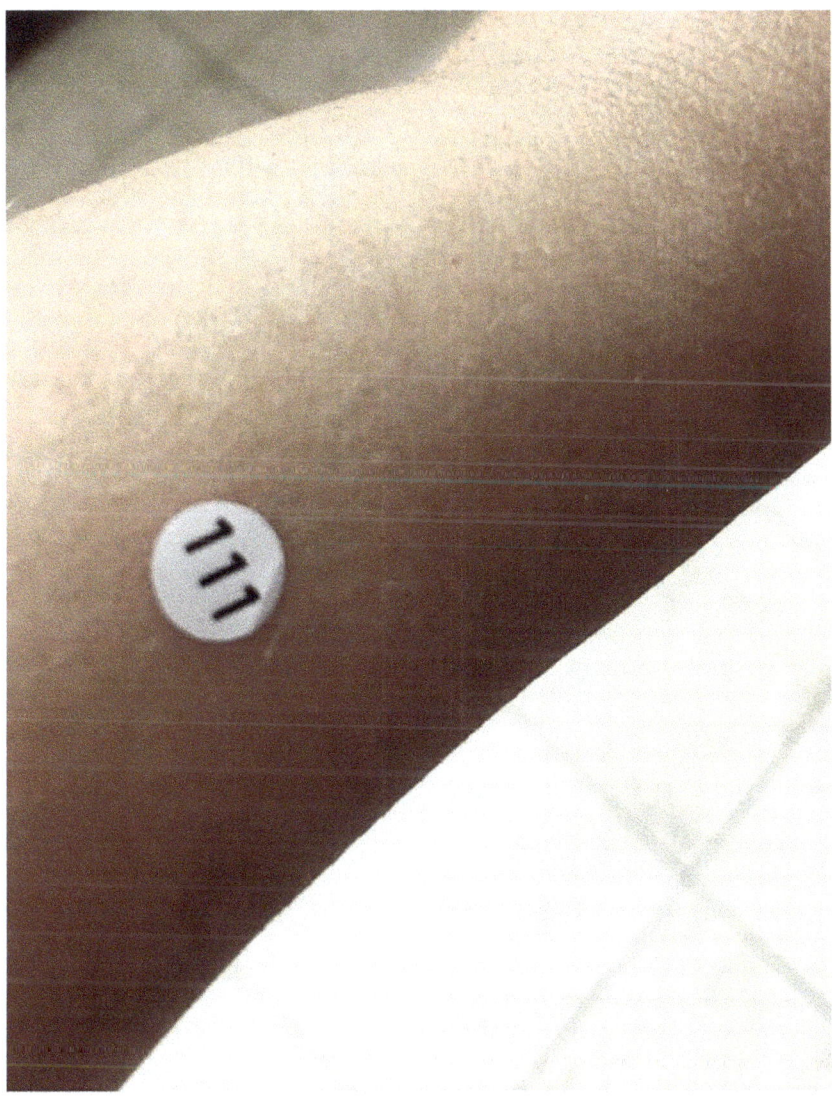

In October 2018, an angel number appeared out of nowhere and was stuck to my arm after a Reiki session. While there are numerous thoughts on what 111 may represent, in this case, I felt it was confirming that it was important to focus on what and how I was thinking, being sure that I was in a positive mindset to manifest what I was trying to achieve.

In May 2016, I stepped back inside after praying and saw that my phone screen was not only displaying 11% charged, but it also happened to be 11:11.

SEE THE SIGNS

When you open up your calculator on your phone and this message appears. I have noticed that both on my phone and on my computer that when my battery- literally and figuratively- need charging as in the both the phone and calculator photos the sign 111 appears. 111 can remind me to keep my thoughts in the positive when I am drained and tired.

ORBS OF LIGHT

Let nothing dim that light that shines from within.

Maya Angelou

You may, at one time or another, find yourself seeing an unexpected object in your photos, videos, or even right in front of you. The object may appear as floating balls of light or orbs. While there has been much debate about what these orbs are, in some cases they are thought to represent angels or our deceased loved ones.

For the story and photos, I am about to share with you, I believe that the orbs are the energy manifested of a beloved deceased family member.

Is there a sign you've received that you can share with me or those you love?

Are you uncomfortable with seeing signs?

Have you allowed yourself to be vulnerable and share a sign you've received with others?

I support you 100% and encourage you to take action today.

Pami's Message

I find myself having to take a moment to breathe in and out a few times to be able share this story with you. It started back on July 17, 1976, when I was seven years old. On that day, I distinctly recall our yellow rotary phone ringing and my mom walking over to answer it. The phone was one with a long, long, long cord, if you know you know, which my mom was using to her advantage and walking into another room. And in a blink of an eye, the sound of heartbreaking crying began. I instantly knew what news was being shared. After a battle with aplastic anemia, my best friend Pami had gained her angel wings.

Pami and I had often walked home from school together, actually many times running home from boys chasing us. We played in the woods behind my grandmother's home and hers, which were adjacent to each other. We were in Brownies together. We visited the neighbors up and down the block, went to the playground, ran around and played outdoor games, and enjoyed carefree days as kids together. And now she was gone.

As anyone could imagine, losing my best friend was devastating. Unfathomable. Life altering. As a child, it was hard for me to comprehend the finality of her being in heaven and not here on earth. I'd been fully aware of her illness, yet praying for her made me believe she would be healed. At that age, I didn't realize how short life could be. Living in a small and connected community, Pami and her family remained near and dear to our heart. Pami's mom, Delphine, became my confirmation sponsor, and I was Delphine's helper for Vacation Bible School. The family continued to live adjacent to my grandmother until my grandmother moved to an apartment later in her life.

Fast-forward to 2016 or 2017. I'm not sure of the exact date, but I do know that I began to have dreams of Pami in a field surrounded by yellow flowers. In my dreams, I would see Pami with her beautiful blonde hair and wide smile. She was glowing amid the vast field of yellow. I felt as if she was trying to relay a message to me, but I wasn't sure exactly what it was.

The dreams came so frequently that I felt the need to reach out to her sister, Jodi Graff Kurtz. Initially, I was hesitant to contact her. Jodi is a beautiful soul inside and out. She was kind and open minded, but I wasn't sure of how she would react to my dream. Would she believe me? Would she understand the message? Would she be sad? Or would she think I was crazy?

I sat with it for a few days, but then Pami appeared in my dreams once again, and I knew I had to reach out to Jodi. With the ease of social media, I had no excuses not to share this. I messaged Jodi, slowly asked her questions, and finally shared my experience.

I'm delighted that I decided to reach out to Jodi. She replied immediately. Not only did Jodi not dismiss my dreams, but she told me that she also believes in signs. More remarkably, she had photos of a sunflower field with an orb of light, which she believed was her sister. It was confirmation that Pami was indeed sharing something with me to share with Jodi and her family.

While some signs may be just for you alone, I've come to realize that sometimes we're given signs to share with others—to comfort them, to remind them, or to confirm that our loved ones are still with us, sometimes in ways we may be surprised to learn about. You may sometimes be scared to talk about signs or perhaps even scared of the signs themselves. Once you embrace your ability to see and believe in signs, however, the more regularly they appear. And the more they appear, the more comfortable you become sharing them with others.

These photos not only contain an orb of light, but there is also an angel figure created by the clouds. These photos not only were taken on multiple occasions but by two different phones.

PETS AND TODDLERS

> Out of the mouths of babes
>
> -Derived from Psalms 8:2

Some people believe that pets and young children have a heightened sensitivity or intuition that allows them to perceive or sense the presence of deceased loved ones or spirits.

In the case of pets such as dogs or cats, accounts suggest that they may exhibit behaviors that indicate an awareness of or interaction with those loved ones. This could include staring at seemingly empty spaces, barking or meowing at something unseen or displaying an unusual behavior.

Similarly, toddlers and young children may exhibit behaviors or make comments that seem to indicate their recognition or communication with deceased loved ones. They may talk about seeing or playing with someone who has passed away, mention specific details about them or exhibit emotions or behaviors that are reminiscent of their interactions with the departed individual.

Has a family pet or young child ever acted as if there was a loved one present?

Did you believe what they were saying or brush it off?

Was their unseen presence a sign for you?

My daughter's Christmas puppy, Emery. December 2011.

Emery had not been a member of our house for long when he developed an interesting routine: After supper, he would suddenly sit in position as if someone was commanding him to sit. Then he would begin barking, growling, and moving toward something. Forward and backward, forward again and backward again. It was as if he was following someone's lead. There was no one visible to our family's eye, but was there someone there? Suddenly, it was as if Emery was trying to jump up and get a treat from someone's hand, as if someone was waving a treat in front of him, saying, "Come and get it!" Eventually, he would sit back down nicely and relax (as seen in the above photo).

One night my husband at the time said, "That's my dad playing with him." Sure enough, Emery got all excited and ran in circles around the island in our kitchen as if in confirmation. We believe my late father-in-law was welcoming Emery into our home and letting us know he was with us and approved—and of course, causing some fun and trouble from beyond.

Mimi's Mom Has Wings

My mom loved being a grandmother of eleven and great-grandmother of two. Due to the pandemic and the fact that she lived out of state, she met my two-and-a-half-year-old granddaughter, Olivia, in person only three times. However, they did Facetime frequently, so she could see how the great-grandchildren were quickly growing and changing.

It was a total surprise that less than twenty-four hours after my mom passed, Olivia was in her room and looked at her mother (my daughter Briana) and said, "Mimi's mom has wings." (Mimi is the name my granddaughter calls me.) My daughter had not shared with her children what had happened, as we all were in such a state of shock from the loss.

Later that morning, Olivia brought her stuffed pink flamingo to their playroom and repeatedly said to Briana, "Mimi mom wings. Mimi mom mingo." She kept showing Briana that pink flamingo to make sure she understood that mom had passed and now had her wings. The stuffed pink flamingo never left her side for weeks. She slept with it and carried it everywhere. She insisted on bringing it on the airplane and to the church where the funeral was held.

After the funeral, we gathered at a family member's house. A pink rocking chair that had been my mom's was brought out for Olivia to take a picture in it (a tradition with the grandkids). Much to our dismay, Olivia refused to sit in the rocking chair. She only wanted the stuffed flamingo in it, stating, "Mimi's mom sit."

I find it so amazing that my grandmother and I had a pink flamingo as my sign from her and now, out of the nowhere, my grandchild and my mother now have the same sign. There really is no explanation except belief that my mom had come to her and let her know she'd crossed over and was still looking after her.

What a comfort, knowing that our children are so tapped in to the energy of others that they can receive messages with such clarity that they can take those messages and relay them to adults. As the scriptures say, out of the mouths of babes. Those babes often surprise us with unexpected wisdom and insight.

Piper's Signs

Piper, a white Labrador, was the happiest when she spent time with her humans. Piper, Maureen, and her husband were a close-knit family. There was a happiness that was beyond description when they all were together. Piper played various roles in her family, including protector, hunting companion, and late-night walking partner. While her affection wasn't the excited, in-your-face type, her presence was often described as regal. Her wise demeanor and calm soul exuded love. She was stationed right next to Maureen at all times. In times of illness, she never veered from watching over her human momma. She was often regarded as an angel dog. She was never in need of anything. Actually, it was like she was there to take care of her beautiful humans.

After fifteen beautiful years, Piper passed away in Maureen's arms in May 2021. As Piper's soul left her body, Maureen and her husband looked up and saw a cardinal looking right at them. The bird stared back at them and connected with them for an extended period of time. It was surely a sign.

While spending time in Florida during that winter, Maureen was feeling especially lonely one day. Hoping to shake up her emotions, she drove to the beach. As she was walking along, the beautiful sunlight was shining on one particular white shell. Maureen just knew this was a sign, a message for her that Piper was walking alongside her just as she did on earth. The shell even looked like angel wings—half of the shell one wing and the sand with the shell design another wing.

On the way back to her car, Maureen crossed paths with a couple who were walking a white lab, just like Piper. To top it off, the couple also happened to be from the area in Minnesota where Maureen lived.

When we're grieving or in distress, signs can come to us whether we're looking for them or not. Have you considered the fact that your pet or beloved animals can send you signs? What sign would you like to receive from your beloved animal angels?

SIGNS OF PROTECTION

> *For he will put his angels in charge of you,*
> *To guard you in all your ways.*

Psalms 91:11

The unexplainable. Plane delayed. The car won't start. Your path is blocked, and you are forced to go another direction. Your garage door breaks, and you cannot leave. A job opportunity doesn't come through as expected. A person you were supposed to meet cancels at the last minute. Walking away from a crash without a scratch on you while there's no clear reasoning how you survived. These are a few scenarios where you may have been protected from something that wasn't for your highest good, averting danger or accidents, maybe even the unfathomable.

Guardian angels, ancestors and ancestral spirits, deities or divine beings are all associated with benevolent entities that offer assistance and protection from beyond the physical realm. They may communicate and provide guidance through intuitive nudges, inner thoughts, or feelings. Additionally assisting individuals make wise choices and avoid harm, help individuals find solutions to problems and provide comfort during challenging times.

June of 2015, my son and I were driving through multiple states, pondering the outcome of an uncertain situation. I was praying for hours during this time, asking for strength for myself and my family. Prayers for answers.

During this drive, I took this photo. Do you see the cross captured perfectly in the rearview mirror of my car that evening? Once this photo was captured, I surrendered and knew that God had the situation under control.

Sure enough, the situation turned around and ended up well. Beyond well. Some people may have looked in the mirror that evening and said, "The sun is in my eyes," and turned away. Yet if you paused just long enough and had an open mind, you might have seen the sign of the cross that I saw.

Have you ever experienced divine intervention?

Was there a time you didn't listen to internal guidance and the result ended in an unfortunate situation?

WORDS OF AFFIRMATION

Kind words can be short and easy to speak, but their echoes are truly endless.

– Mother Teresa

Words of affirmation are a form of communication that involves expressing affection, appreciation, positivity and support through spoken or written words. They are a way to uplift and encourage and can have a powerful impact on our emotional well-being. Receiving or hearing positive words can be comforting and meaningful. During times of grief and longing for connection from loved ones who have passed away or your divine creator, there are signs or messages that you are sending you. Whether your life is in balance or not, words of affirmation can reinforce the positive and inspire you to conquer the negative. To keep going no matter what.

Words of affirmation can be signs found on license plates, billboards, magazines, social media or even during conversations with friends or family. If you are not spotting words of affirmation out in the wild, one of the fun things I like to do is open a book, magazine or newspaper to a random page and see what message appears to me on that page. I generally take a moment and ask that whatever I need to hear, I am guided to. Then I open the book up on what page feels "right." Try this with this book. When you are finished reading it, or even right now, ask what message you need to hear today and concentrate on what page to open it up to. What was the theme of the page? Is it a sign that you need to pay attention to? You can also do this with a deck of cards such as oracle cards. Concentrate on your question, shuffle the cards, and then pull a card out for your guidance.

Your order has been paid for. I am always shocked and full of gratitude when I hear these words. This can happen to you when you are at a drive through and the customer in front of you pays for your order! Maybe you have been asking for a sign to feel more loved or feel more financially abundant. What inspired the person in front of you to give you a gift or pay it forward? Maybe they are listening to the nudges they are receiving.

I have experienced many words of affirmation throughout the years appearing when I needed them. While I'd love to share the stories behind what was happening when I captured these photos, I've decided these words and photos are for you to soak up today. To determine what they mean to you. In what circumstances would have hoped these words would have shown up for you and be your sign?

When you see words of affirmation, take a photo.

Affirm your connection to the message by stating the words out loud.

Share words of affirmation, your message may be the sign someone needs to hear today.

YOUR PART

Your journey here is yours, uniquely yours. Wonderfully yours. Amazingly yours. Yet, at some point days may be filled with uncertainty, sadness, confusion, grief, anxiousness. You are here to experience life. And some days, boy, do we ever feel the experiences of life.

When the unseen world reaches out to you, to connect with you, to offer comfort and reassurance, be present with an open heart and open mind.

Trust your intuition. Learn to listen to your inner voice, your knowing. Pay attention to the subtle nudges, gut feelings or ah ha moments that arise from within. These whispers can guide you to the signs you seek.

Be open to seeing signs in various forms.

Be patient as signs come in their own time.

Connect through ritual. Create your own personal ritual such as lighting a candle, meditating, journaling, or visiting a special space that keeps your energy in tune and invite signs into your life.

Invite communication in by speaking to your deceased loved ones, God, angels, whatever your beliefs are. Share your thoughts, feelings and desires and trust they hear you.

Practice gratitude. Take time to acknowledge and appreciate the signs that have touched your life. Gratitude opens the door wider for further signs to emerge, creating connection.

See The Signs.

May your journey be filled with experiences creating belief, providing hope and affirming connection.

SIGN STORIES

I believe that sharing our stories can be a powerful catalyst for healing and hope.

That is why I am extending an invitation to each one of you to reach out to me via email: info@KimberlyBrazier.com and share your own sign stories and photos. Whether it's a subtle sign, a vivid dream or an uncanny synchronicity, I would LOVE to hear about the signs that have touched your lives and brought you moment of: creating belief, providing hope and affirming connection.

By sharing your stories, we create a community of connection. Of understanding. Of knowing. We are not alone in our experiences.

I will be looking to speak with individuals on my podcast and future books. Will this be you? Let me know!

If you want support, I am here. Here to listen, guide, coach, and hold space. Please connect via my private sessions on my website and see my past work experiences. I can't wait to meet you!

www.seethesignsbook.com
or www.KimberlyBrazier.com

Much love,
Kimberly

JOURNAL

Reflect on a specific sign or message you received from your loved one recently.
What was the context it occurred?
How did it align with a current situation or challenge you were facing?
What insights or guidance did you gain from this sign?

*Think about a cherished memory or characteristic of your loved ones.
How have your seen this particular trait or memory manifest in your life?
Are there any recurring signs or synchronicities that remind you of them?
How often do these experiences impact your sense of connection or healing?*

Consider a time when you were seeking guidance, confirmation, or support.
Did you ask for a sign?
Did you receive any specific signs in response?
Reflect on the significance of those signs and how the influenced your decisions, provided comfort or direction during that period.

Sign Tracker- document when and which signs you encounter.

SEE THE SIGNS

www.ingramcontent.com/pod-product-compliance
Lightning Source LLC
Chambersburg PA
CBHW070500100426
42743CB00010B/1699